PAEAN

KENNETH LEIGHTON

This work was given its first performance by Simon Preston in the Royal Festival Hall, London, on 25 January 1967 (the 40th anniversary of The Organ Club): he has recorded it on Argo ZRG 528 (stereo) RG 528 (mono). Duration 4½ minutes.

OXFORD UNIVERSITY PRESS, MUSIC DEPARTMENT, GREAT CLARENDON STREET, OXFORD OX2 6DP